Forever Laid Formula

Best Ways To Get Women To Sleep With You

Taylor Timms

Author Online!

For updates and more
seduction resources visit
Taylor Timms page at

www.foreverlaid.com

Forever Laid Formula:
Best Ways To Get Women To Sleep With You
by **Taylor Timms**

ISBN 978-0-9866004-2-5

Printed in the United States of America

Version 1.2

Free Online Seduction Course

As a thank you for buying this book, I would like to give you access to my on-line seduction course.

To claim your free spot, please go to
www.foreverlaid.com
and enter your valid email address now.

Also by Taylor Timms

Top Bikini Pictures
ISBN 978-0-9866426-3-0

Beautiful Breasts Pictures
ISBN 978-1-926917-01-6

Sexy Butt Pictures
ISBN 978-1-926917-15-3

Best Gift Ideas For Women
ISBN 978-0-9866004-4-9

See all books here:
http://astore.amazon.com/taylortimms-20

Congratulations!

Congratulations on your purchase of the Forever Laid Formula! By purchasing this book you are basically telling me that you're ready to increase the amount of women you are capable of picking up - and that these women are increasingly attractive.

This is the first step of many.

Although this is the most important step - getting your hands on amazing information on how to get laid more, there will be lots of things you must do on your own.

But as promised I am going to take you by the hand and give you all the information I've learned on how to consistently get laid by beautiful women.

Note: This book/guide call it what you want, is different than all others in that it actually provides you with facts and tips learned from my past experiences. I'm not going fill this book up with fluff and 'hear-say'. So enjoy the fruits of my labor!

This guide is going to teach you psychological things about women that will help you seduce them. This guide will also give you a ton of things that you need to work on yourself.

This guide differs for that reason... not only will you learn all about women and what they are looking for, but you'll learn how to better mold yourself into something that they naturally like... making it easier on you.

WARNING: Before we go any further let me tell you this. I may be able to pick up women at whim, but writing is NOT my thing. I decided against hiring someone else to write this for me because it wouldn't have meant so much to me… so that means YOU will just have to deal with how I write. Got it… good.

Introduction

I'm thinking that I need to fill you in about me, as every good friend would. You need to know who I am and where I come from so you know that I wasn't born a "stud" or anything like that.

I don't look like Brad Pitt.

I don't have abs like Ryan Reynolds.

And even though I am a fairly successful author of several books, including the one you're reading, I'm not a millionaire.

But before I go further…

…I need to go back in time.

A little anecdote about how I used to be

I was sitting on the steps of my high school. As I sat I was contemplating on how I should go about it, and it hit me… JUST ASK!

I was a junior at the high school. Inexperienced in the way of picking up women or getting numbers. Just plain scared.

But…

Prom was next week and I knew the girl I had liked since 8th grade still had no date. I thought for sure I could ask and she'd say "yes", even if it was for pity… I didn't care!

So I sat and sat waiting for her to come out of class so I could snatch this opportunity and go to prom with the girl of my dreams. I'm telling you... long dark hairs, dark eyes, beautiful smile... everything I wanted and more.

Then, she was there.

20 feet from me – coming down the stairs.

I was nervous and the palms were sweaty, but nothing was going to stop me from asking her and getting this date!

I walked up beside her and said, "Hey Emily"

"Hi" she smiled back.

"So I was wondering...um..." I hesitated,

"What is it?" she insisted.

"Would you come with me to the prom... like as a date?" I smiled as my stomach wrenched and the air from my lungs disappeared.

"Well..." she said. "I'm actually going stag with Betsy... and we kinda talked about it already. Sorry" smiling as she walked away.

"Oh OK, well talk to you later." I said. I was about to die.

After walking to my car I couldn't understand it. She would rather go by herself than have a date?

The End!

And that's how it was for the remainder of high school and through most of college. Absolutely no luck with women and frustrated as hell sexually!

The Break - Through

The break through came from my senior year in college.

Here I was a Psychology Major – so I was learning all about how people work and interact with each other AND why they do it. I then started paying closer attention to what I was learning… and paying attention to people or being more observational one might say.

Also, luckily for me…

I started hanging out with a couple guys from a class who so happened to be absolute masters at picking up women. One of the guys, who I'll call Brett, could literally pick up girls anywhere!

We could be out picking up groceries – he'd pick up a girl.

We could be at a bar – he'd pick up a girl and get a minimum of 5 numbers.

We could even be at the library – and somehow Brett could pull a number or pick up a girl! Amazing!

So these are the two things that made the biggest impact on my life and the amount I get laid to this day. By becoming more observational and getting first hand knowledge straight from two guys that could pick up girls at anytime.

After hanging out with them for awhile I started trying more and more to hit on women anytime I could. The more you try the better you get was my train-of-thought. Practice makes perfect!

So I kept trying new things. Going to new places. Starting off with different tones and pitches to my voice. I went crazy!

I literally had turned this into a scientific experiment. Granted I was motivated to keep trying for one reason only: TO GET LAID!

That was the goal of my tireless efforts.

I wanted to know what would work and what definitely didn't work. I wanted to be able to be at any place and any time and have an extremely good chance of getting a phone number and then getting laid. That's it!

NOTE! If you are looking for a long-term relationship you may want to read my book on dating! This guide is really for those trying to learn to pick up women and get laid.

BUT…it doesn't hurt still knowing how to attract and seduce women even if you're looking for something long-term. One of the girls you successfully pick up could be the next Mrs. YOU.

Or you may find a girl you really, genuinely care for and need to know how to get her to like you sexually back. Or to get her number… TO MAKE THE FIRST STEP!

So either way… you might as well keep reading and learn something.

OK, back to me in college;

So after months of exhaustive trying to pick up as many girls as possible I stumbled upon it. I realized that in one weekend I had gotten 10 phone numbers and gotten laid by two different women.

I'm not trying to brag – that's not the point. I'm just stating that those are good numbers for one weekend and it shows that something is going right.

So I back-tracked on everything that was going on.

What I wore. How I acted. Who I approached and when.

After I did that for a day or two, I started connecting the dots. I started seeing what I was doing right and I created the ideas in my head so I could use them everyday.

I of course implemented these techniques the following weekend... with even better results.

I finally cracked the code. The "get-laid-by-beautiful-women-even-though-I'm-not-rich,-ripped, - or Brad Pitt" code. Kinda long I know... but that pretty much is the code right there.

Enough of me boring you with my stories. I'll use previous experiences throughout this book, but for now let's jump into it. I'm excited!

You'd better be dammit! Let's go show you how to get laid!

The Layout of this Book - and Why

So I've decided to lay this book out without any "chapters", but instead to use a "sectional" theme. It's mainly going to focus on two things: YOU and HER. By HER I mean every women.

I'm also going to be laying out details on techniques to use and even things I'll call experiments – but we'll get to that later.

Before I go any further... now is the time to decide.

Decide that this is what you want. You want to start improving your chances of getting laid and getting numbers. You NEED to WANT this.

BOTTOM LINE - you need to stop being a pansy; take everything you learn here and actually apply it! Do not let this become a paper weight! Do not!

For god's sake...READ. LEARN. USE.

Section 1:

YOU

From the book 'Top Bikini Pictures'. Check out the book for over 100 color bikini pictures:
http://astore.amazon.com/taylortimms-20

You may be wondering, "Wait a minute. Aren't I supposed to be learning about women and how they work?"

The answer is: YES

But first we need to start changing you. We need to make sure you have all your cards-in-a-row so that when it comes time to make your moves, it's not just an epic fail.

Learning about how to mold you into something a woman would be attracted to is the first and MOST IMPORTANT STEP. Even all the game in the world can't help you if you don't have the initial qualities that women seek.

Ready?

Go to the next page – if you haven't realized yet that I'm trying to motivate you to succeed than you might as well just give up on women all-together!

What?

You haven't given up? Excellent.

Section 1.1

Trust me, there is a need for change!

Obviously there's a need for change; you're here right? You wouldn't be here if you were already a master at picking up women. You also wouldn't be here if you were a happily married man who already had is fun.

No.

You're here because you need help.

You need guidance from someone with experience and who wants to see you succeed. You know that you're not the best at picking up women. You know so much that you are willing to put everything on the line, purchase this book, and make a change in your life.

That's what I want to hear.

That kind of motivation or realization that "Hey, maybe it's time I seek help!" is what will drive a man to change. This is how things get accomplished.

It takes some relinquishment of pride!

That's right!

It's time to realize that you aren't as good as you think. The first step that I learned while improving these skills, believe me – they're skills, is that you have to be able to admit that you're just not that good with women.

I actually have taught seminars on subjects like this, and men can never admit that they're not good with women. You have to get past the pride. You have to just realize that your methods aren't working well enough and you'll open your mind up to something new. Something fresh!

Change is inevitable.

Being able to change and improve yourself to meet higher standards is something that isn't frowned upon. You shouldn't feel bad that you're taking advice from someone on how to pick up women. You should be proud that you're not being passive anymore... BUT instead being active on improving your life – especially sexually.

So we've established that there is a need for change right?

Like I said!

You're here because you want to be able to pick up more women. Get more numbers and get more women into bed with you… and I think you're ready for the change!

Section 1.2

Walk the Walk

Now that we've decided you need the change, and we've "talked-the-talk"… let's get on to the more important step in changing you. Taking the walk!

In order to push you to change we need to do some things first:

First we need to MAKE GOALS. We need to define where you're going or what you want out of this book. So let's talk about that first.

What do you want from this guide? From me? From yourself?

I think you need to take a second and think… "How many women do I want to pick up?"

Here's your second ……………… thousand one!

OK.

So now that we've figured out that you need to improve the number of women you get numbers from and the number you ultimately sleep with, our goal is set.

We'll start with the goal that we need to:

AT LEAST DOUBLE THE AMOUNT OF WOMEN YOU CURRENTLY SLEEP WITH.

Note: This may not be that hard of a goal. If you slept with 5 or less women last year, I want you to shoot for at least 3 times that number! But we'll get to all that later.

So our goal is set.

Now you're feeling it right? The blood flowing. The excitement that you will actually improve your "numbers". Hell, I'm excited for you!

ON THIS NOTE: On the note of setting goals, let me remind you that the goal we choose is of course not a set goal. If you are going to completely pass this goal then by all means, allow yourself to do that.

Also, don't let yourself feel tied down to the goal; when we have that pressure of 'needing' to meet a quota, we become nervous and less effective. The goal is only for motivation... I actually expect you to do better than it anyway!

Unrealistic expectations

Make sure when you set a goal that it's not unrealistic.

First, don't tell yourself that you want to get laid by 10x as many women this year than last. Chances are that won't happen. It's going to take time for you to start introducing techniques and for your confidence to build.

Also if you set a standard that is too high and you don't meet it you'll become discouraged and just give up. Believe me when I say this...

...YOU WILL BE REJECTED FROM TIME TO TIME - IT COMES WITH THE TERRITORY!

So if you have a couple bad nights you don't just give up! You get back out there and try again.

Another common pitfall in making progress and changing things is that we guys tend to analyze things too much.

They say that men are the rational creatures and women are the emotional ones: well it's true!

When we start thinking about change we can sometimes get "too" caught up in all the little things. We over-analyze ourselves which always leads to a loss in confidence, which again we'll get to later.

Another thing you'll have to watch out for is that you don't think you're a master if you happen to pick a woman up! Seriously... don't let this happen. You must never let your shoes get too big that you can't fill them.

By letting this happen you'll be skipping steps that are really important to getting laid. AGAIN, don't ever think you've learned everything. After all my years of success in dating and getting laid, I still understand that I don't know a whole lot.

So, now we've seen you need some change. We've made some goals and I suggested some things for you to watch out for. Let's get to the important things: What actually needs to change.

Section 1.3
The Changes

Another thing that will separate this book from any other is that I'm going to give you actual advice that I've learned from women throughout the years. Also, this advice is the same stuff I started changing when I decided to start getting laid more.

So instead of filling your head up with 'fluff', I'm actually going to give you real, concrete pointers that are necessary in your overall success.

I'm going to use a recent study done by Synovate, which asked 250 women to mention what makes men desirable, and here were the results.

1. Good Hygiene
2. Confidence
3. A Great Smile
4. Strong Fashion Sense
5. A tough or macho look

So I'm going to use these as the basis for my explanation on what you need to change... or not.

Hygiene

For the love of god, or whatever deity you're into these days you must always clean yourselves!

Shower daily or more if you workout more than once. Brush your teeth at least twice a day; invest in teeth whitening or whitening-style toothpaste. Trim facial hair – huge beards don't attract women.

Keep your hair nicely done, because although some women don't mind the "messy" look you're better off sticking to something that is clean and proper. If you do choose to have long hair well then take care of it, you're not a rock star so you can't just let it do whatever.

Here comes something I hate, but it's true...moisturize! Use lotion. That's right! Use it on your hands after you shower. Believe me, I have had many women compliment my soft hands and although that may sound strange, trust me – it's good. Try it out.

Other hygiene issues, wash your clothes regularly like mom taught you to. You should also iron shirts with collars before going out... but we'll save the clothes for the good fashion sense section coming up.

Did I miss anything?

Let's see... oh yeah, no uni-brows! Seriously, you can't rock it!

Shave, wax, I don't care, there is supposed to be skin between them!

Also make sure you wear deodorant. You're probably laughing but some of you slack on this one; you should "generously" apply this ok.

One last trick for your personal hygiene. If you're going to a club, consider applying baby-powder to certain areas that may receive more sweat than others... just do it, seriously. Many guys already know to do this, but a lot still don't remember that if you're trying to get laid this is something she'll appreciate!

CONFIDENCE
Head up!

Having confidence is something that I can't just tell you and you'll get.

You have to honestly believe in yourself and your capabilities or your "value" for you to display confidence.

The thing I don't understand is that you should already be confident. You're probably a good guy, got a job, have friends – so why not have confidence?

Most guys are afraid that they're not good enough for the woman they want to approach... and let me be the first to tell you that YOU ARE.

No matter how much I re-assure you though I just can't help in this department. I can give you all the tools and tell you that there's nothing to be afraid of when approaching a woman, but it's up to you to believe me.

A couple things on confidence:

Exercise
Not only do women appreciate a man with a decent physique, but it also helps you build confidence. Have you ever left the gym not

feeling confident?

Seriously?

When is the last time you pumped some iron or did some cardio and left the gym with your head hanging down? Never.

Exercise makes you feel alive and more in control of you and any situation. It's proven to release the hormones that ramp your libido and your confidence in yourself. So if you're not on an exercise program of some sort than you'd better start... it'll pay dividends I promise.

If you don't then here's a sample workout to start you off:

4 days a week to start

Monday - Run (at least 30 minutes)

Tuesday - Weights
     Chest – bench 3 X 10
     Back – Pull downs – 3 X 10
     Biceps – Curls – 3 X 10
     Triceps – Dips – 3 X 10
     Legs – Squats – 3 X 10
     Don't forget calves – 3 X 10

Abs - your choice, but feel the burn!

Thursday - Run

Friday - Repeat Tuesday (vary workout choices)

Now this isn't a hardcore program by no means, but if you're just starting out than try it out for a few weeks and then switch it up.

I cannot stress enough how great exercise is to improving your confidence.

One more thing with confidence:

To those of you with "standards", it may be time for you to think about things differently.

I am about to enlighten you to something I learned many years ago when it comes to getting laid by hot women... you need practice.

You need to occasionally try picking up women whom you know you can – I'm talking women who most would consider "not attractive".

Now you're probably thinking, "what?!"

I don't blame you!

This is just a technique I have used a few times over the years if I was feeling rusty, and it is by all means OPTIONAL! I just have learned that it is easier to talk to these type of women and work on your humor and other things that you'll be able to use when searching for hotter women.

Again: optional, but it's helped me in the past and it could help you... just thought I should mention it.

A Great Smile

I don't think I need to elaborate much on this one.

Use whitening toothpaste or strips. If you're teeth are seriously out-of-whack, get them fixed.

The key here is that whenever you're at a bar, club, anywhere... you want to smile! Women want to see you having fun and they want to see a smile .

Back when I was first 21 and still not good at getting laid, I would never smile when at a bar. I actually didn't know this at the time but was fortunate to meet a young woman who actually said she thought I was "cute" but I never smiled, and that I should because women will like it more.

That's how I learned – embarrassing at the time, maybe. Good to know – absolutely.

SMILE!

Strong Fashion Sense
Let's see that wardrobe! I'm sure you think you're an 'ok' dresser but I doubt you are.

Right now we're changing things about you, and your clothes are probably something that needs improved. Time to go find a men's magazine like GQ and see what's popular right now.

The single best way to do this is take a sister or a friend who is a woman and simply ask for help picking things out.

Not only will they have a blast, but you'll get great advice from a woman. Make sure she's around the same age of the women you intend on picking up because women's opinion on what's in style changes with.

If you're looking to pick up women below 30, make sure they're below 30 - simple.

Make sure you get shoes also.

The three basic colors to make sure to have are brown, black, and white. Tan can also come in handy as well.

Again I can't help tremendously with this one because I can't go shopping with you, but I can tell you that the best way is to have a woman come with.

Remember: Don't get caught wearing brown anything if you're shirt is black! I've had women tell me this and it's a little embarrassing – double check. This goes for the opposite too; no black if you're shirt is brown OR dark blue. Ask a girl!

Macho look
I won't go into this at all. Exercise and just don't act like a little girl... that's pretty straight-forward.

Watch some Sylvester Stallone movies, that'll show you macho!

Well that's all the changes that you need to consider starting today. Those are the physical or appearance changes you need to live by.

NOW ON TO THE WOMAN SECTION!

Section 2

The Woman

**Remember that women are
not "impossible" to figure out.**

Section 2.1

Common misconceptions about women

The "Pedestal Problem"

The Pedestal Problem is the most common problem of men like you and like the old me. We always find ourselves digging up our little insecurities and the "you're not good enough" thoughts that will always spoil your chances.

Men who haven't gained that confidence that I talked about earlier will continue to put women on a pedestal – a place where they can't reach. Not only is that completely backwards from the truth, but you're setting yourself for failure.

Always be KNOWING, not even thinking, KNOWING that you can obtain any hot girl you choose. That's what I'm trying to help you with.

Also there are other little things that come with the Pedestal Problem that I need to share with you. These are misconceptions that lead men to feeling insecure, afraid, and less confident.

I'll state each one and then I'll immediately respond with what is the truth. Pay attention!

- **I need to approach women, because if I don't I'm a loser.**

First of all, yes you will need to approach women because this is all part of the process of building your confidence and getting face time with as many women as possible. The problem is that if you're out one night and aren't feeling it, it's ok to not approach women. Having this pressure to approach women causes anxiety and stress which leads to more problems with your confidence.

If you haven't figured it out yet, confidence is a big factor in your success in getting laid more. Most things will lead to that so stay focused.

- **I need to convince her that I'm a worthy partner.**

No, you don't. You never want to go to a woman thinking you have to convince her. You need to be focused on making the changes I mentioned earlier and you will be worthy. Thinking like this get's guys feeling like they're already a lower class than who they're approaching. Ties in with the pedestal theory.

- **If I get rejected, it's going to be a big deal and I'll feel bad about myself.**

Again, you're unknowingly placing her on a pedestal so that if she happens to say "No thanks", you take this as a sign of SERIOUS DEFEAT and your confidence drops. Reality needs to be that if she rejects you than its HER LOSS! There are plenty of other beautiful women who will dig you.

- **I need to impress her or let her dictate what happens.**

No no no! You don't need to impress her in any other way than being yourself; well the new and improved you. Also, remember that you're the one dictating where this goes. You show her that you're the boss and she'll repay you.

- **Being nice to her is what she wants, I need to compliment her several times.**

I've actually had women tell me that it's creepy when men are overly nice and compliment too much. Later on we'll get on the actual approach of a woman and what techniques to use, but for now know that 1 compliment is far enough when trying to get laid. Just one.

Those very common misconceptions are the things that tie into the Pedestal Problem, you place the woman above you already making her impossible to reach. No woman...I mean NO woman is out of your reach!

Section 2.2

Things you should know about women - basics.

Women are like you – they DO enjoy sex.

It's true.

I know you're thinking, if they enjoy it so much than why don't they go out and pick up guys on a regular basis all on-their-own?

Some do... but those are scarce creatures.

Women tend to not pick up guys for sex regularly when they could because of the problem I'll label as "The Societal Condition".

The Societal Condition

So us men, we have it easy… we can go to a bar, pick up a woman, have sex with her, and the expect absolutely nothing out of it as far as long-term relationships. We're lucky!

Society has programmed everyone to just "know" and "expect" for many single men to do this. Maybe labeled as "players" or other terms, but the great thing is that people don't actually look down on us for doing it.

It just seems natural.

Now women… oh lord, they can't just do that. No no no!

If women take that route and do the same things we do, like sleep with men and actually ENJOY sex for the sake of sex… they get negative labels such as:

"Slut"
"Whore"
"Tramp"

You've heard them all before right?

These labels unfortunately have a more negative impact on the female and her "social" position.

See women depend more on how society views them than us guys. It's just one little issue that's came up through "The Societal Condition", but don't worry…

...we can get past this! We can get the woman to realize her inner-true, incredibly-sexual self. I will show you how!

To start with, you as a man, need to remember that every girl that you approach – that deep down inside she is AS SEXUAL/ OR MORE SEXUAL of a creature than you are. Deep down underneath her "fakeness" that she puts on for public display, is a woman who loves sex – bottom line.

The trick is to get past this – to make her want sex without feeling like a "slut".

Another issue that gets in the way of a woman wanting to have sex with you is the fact that sex was designed for one thing in mind: Procreation.

The woman knows that there is the danger of her getting pregnant and that risk is sometimes enough for her to turn down.

This is why the first step in getting in bed with a woman is to not verbalize anything about sex – why? Because "The Societal Condition" will kick in and she'll start thinking "Am I a Slut?" "What if I get pregnant?"

Two things she doesn't need to worry about – so don't push her.

Never communicated with her your intentions about having sex (that is what this books about) and never tell her about previous scores. Two no-no's.

Section 2.3

Mel Gibson knows!

STOP RIGHT THERE... Time for random facts!

Because this book is about women, and getting into bed with them – I want to not only teach you how but also give you insight into women in general.

The greater you understand women – the better your chances!

These "random facts" are being pulled from data I just found while searching... and I thought it'd be nice to lay'em out here for you to absorb.

Random Facts Table #1

- 24% of women didn't orgasm the last time they had sex. (it's up to you!).
- 28% of women whose last sexual encounter resulted in orgasm from penetration. (good lord don't forget the other parts!).
- 62% of women whose biggest body hang-up is their belly.
- 16% of women whose biggest body hang-up is their thighs.
- 7.5 – the average performance ranking, on a scale of 1-10, that women gave the last man they slept with.
- 5.8 – minimum ranking a man could receive to earn a second engagement.
- 87% of women who are willing to give a man directions in bed.

- 72% of women who says it turns them on when a man helps out around the house (random fact, but not that important to us trying to get laid).
- 32% of women who say doing the dishes is the best way to help (again, not that important – but good to know).

Back to What Women Want!

If you didn't catch on we're talking about what women want and what kind of man they like OR are attracted to – which is where you'll need to be.

Before I fill you in on things women like – which comes mostly from personal experience and some from other sources of research – you need to know that no woman is the same, but they all tend to lean a certain way.

What this means is that if you learn what I'm teaching you and make those necessary changes, you can adapt to any certain woman without any issue.

So first let me tell you that you cannot believe any woman about what she "likes" in a man.

Let's say you have friends that are women and they tell you that they're looking for a really "nice" guy who will take care of them and give them roses every week – you NEED to take a look at who they've been dating.

Never just take a woman's word for it, the proof is in who she's dated. If she's dated nothing but jerks than you know she's into that. So step one is to simply be observant about what

women want and never ever listen to what the
say they want.

You Pursue

Here's another thing a woman wants.

Very few women in all my years of going
out to clubs or parties have ever made the first
move – they just don't do that. Again, back to
the "feeling slutty" thing and how they've been
taught.

This is our job – they love it anyway. So
do it. You be the wolf and let her be the sheep –
this is how she wants it!

You need to make the first move. You need
to move the conversation to where it needs to go
– with confidence. She'll recognize that you're a
man that isn't afraid to pursue.

Not only does she like the chase, but
it makes her feel "special" and "attractive" –
important!

Another important part in what SHE
WANTS is that while your pursuing her you need
to drive her AWAY from what society says about
"being slutty"…

…you need to create an environment where she
feels there won't be any consequences in having
sex with you. So that's why when you pursue
you don't tell her your real focus. Just a reminder
not to be too explicit about your intentions!

Don't be Insecure - or Needy - or Ask Approval!

Now I'm about to really start preaching... so listen up!

Women are insecure – tell me you knew that!

You may have, but didn't realize how important it is to you getting laid. It's definitely one of THE MOST IMPORTANT THINGS TO REMEMBER: WOMEN ARE INCREDIBLY INSECURE.

All women are.

Women are worrying about their hair. How they smell. How their outfits are coordinated. She's sizing up other women... her head is spinning all the time!

So... because women are insecure about themselves – THEY DON'T WANT A MAN IS AS INSECURE AS THEM.

Don't be constantly checking your hair when talking to women. Trust me, if you're talking to that woman – your hair is fine.

Don't ask her things like "Am I boring you?" "I hope I'm not keeping you from anyone?" She doesn't want an insecure wuss.

Also, don't let your insecurities sprout any jealousy issues. This is something that is saved usually for people in relationships but I thought I should mention it anyway.

Other questions to stay away from:

"Am I doing okay?"

"Do you find me attractive?"

Statement like: "Wow, you're really hot!"

"Are you having fun?" - you may think it's ok to ask, but really… it's not.

You get the idea right?

Stray away from questions that ask her if she's ok and things like that. These are definitely hard to stay away from in the beginning – believe me, but once you start practicing more with women you'll never do it again.

From the book 'Beautiful Breasts Pictures'. Check out the book for
over 150 color breast pictures:
http://astore.amazon.com/taylortimms-20

Section 3:

Talking to Women - the Approach

Section 3.1

Your move sucka!

Another great thing about this guide is that no other out there will actually lay out for you the right way to approach women. I am seriously giving you the key's to my kingdom here man – it's enlightenment time baby!

Eye Contact - DON'T BE THE FIRST TO LOOK AWAY!

Let's say you're at a bar and you look down to the end of the bar and an attractive woman is checking you out – what would most men do?

Most men would become insecure and look away first – but not you.

You stare and you smirk or smile until she looks away, and now you're already in control of the tempo of this interaction.

This direct eye contact will not only let her know that you're interested but it will also tell her that you're not afraid of her knowing that you're checking her out.

NOTE: Don't stare like a creepy dude though. When I say look at a woman, you must smile or smirk and if she keeps staring you need to get up and walk to her immediately. Don't have a long staring match. Chances are she'll look away pretty quickly.

Ok, moving on.

As you approach her – remember to smile! Don't be focused on anything else.

I personally will put my Blackberry on silent so that there are no interruptions and I can give her all of my attention.

So now you've arrived to her, what are you going to do now?

"Can I get you something to drink?"

Oldest trick – but it works. It invokes a conversation and this is all you're looking for. If she say's "No, thanks"… and you have some nerve – like me – you'll say, "I'm not asking you to go to Maui for the weekend… it's only a drink".

This shows persistence – but if she says no again then leave and remind her to have a nice night. Maybe if you're lucky she'll drink a few more and remember you showing interest. Hey, that's happened to me before.

Let's say you get her attention and a conversation starts… now what?

So you sit down and order her drink, and yours – don't make her feel as if she's the only one drinking. NOTE: Get a manly drink, no appletinis or anything like that.

Now is when you start talking, but there are things you need to be on the lookout for. The first you'll need to do is make contact and tell her your name – no pickup lines or anything like that. If you tell her that her dad was a thief because he stole the stars and put them in her eyes then you should just say goodnight now!

As you speak you have to remember to slow down.

Learn to articulate your words better. Let those words just flow out of your mouth in a smooth and relaxing way. Also, don't speak with an low voice – that doesn't exude confidence. Speak like you mean it, but don't yell.

Also when you speak there are certain body gestures and mannerisms that you need to stay away from:

1. **Don't speak too quickly** – speak slower. Enunciate your words. Take your time when speaking to her.
2. **Use fluctuations in your voice** – give life to what you say. Have you ever seen the Clear Eyes eyedrops commercial? That guy speaks in what's called a "Monotone" voice – youtube that, and DON'T DO IT because she'll quickly find you boring.
3. **Stay away from things like** "like" "um" and "eh" – be clear about what you're saying.
4. **Move around a lot** – you need to just be relaxed while speaking to her. Don't look away a lot or twitch. This will show her your either not really interested in her or that you're nervous – both of which are bad.
5. **When she asks a question**, answer it right away – waiting too long to answer may show her your not being yourself. Women like spontaneity.
6. **Don't be constantly touching yourself** – don't be rubbing your face or your arm or anything else. What I like to do is keep my hands around my waist somewhere – not in pockets – but just out of the way of her view.
7. **Don't be rigid** – I already mentioned that being relaxed and showing her that you're

comfortable around her displays major confidence and she'll like it.

8. **Don't look down or check your phone** – I decided to put these together because so often people will look down and when they do they pull out their cell phones. This will show her your bored, your insecure, and you're not really there all in one go – and that is just bad. Like I said, I keep my phone on silent and eye contact on her.

9. **While walking to her**, walk with some movement – don't be rigid in the upper part of your body. You want to move around a little, and show some sway. Again this shows the relaxation and confidence.

10. **Try not to blink obsessively** – this is hard to control because some of us blink a lot. You just have to try and remember not to. This could tell her you're bored, tired, or nervous – all of which isn't what you want.

11. **Don't be afraid to touch her** – if you're standing and she makes a joke then touch her shoulder gently while laughing. A gentle touch goes a long way for confidence and comfort around her.

12. **Don't be smart** – we all know that women are intelligent, but don't talk work or any boring theories about evolution.

13. **Don't end your sentences with** "right" or "don't you think so" - this is back to you seeking her approval. She'll think that you're not a confident man that doesn't have his own opinion.

14. While talking to her **don't check out other**

women – seriously… I 'm not even going into this. You know better!

15. **Don't be a "1-upper"** – you ever have a friend that when you tell a story they always have a story that is just better than yours? I'm guessing you have and you know that it's annoying. Don't try and prove you have better stories than her or you're funnier.

Also when speaking to her try and be cocky and funny together. This concept is really hard to explain, but I'll try…

You have to be funny while being a little arrogant. This will show confidence but will help keep her from thinking you're a jerk – although jerks do get laid more than nice guys.

Watch Dane Cook in any of his movies talking to women – seriously!

He does the funny/cocky thing great and you can get real genuine tips from watching him. I did and that's where I learned a few tricks. You can consider it "research".

Touch her!

I'm a real believer that touching is what helps a lot.

If you're walking away for another drink gently touch her hand or shoulder. If she's standing the small of her back will work. Touching again shows that you're not afraid of her and you're confident, but it also will get her thinking about sex.

Never grab her or squeeze anything.

Also when you're talking to the woman and things are going great you also need to give her some compliments – it's something that just needs to happen.

Which do you think is better?

- "You seem really fun. What do you do in your free time?"
- "Wow you're hot. Do you work out a lot?"

You think I'm joking right?!

I'm not. I've actually heard guys use a compliment like this before and it doesn't go over well. Keep your compliments to her personality, but if you want to say she looks hot, say…

"You look amazing tonight. Do you look this amazing every night or is it just Saturdays?" She'll laugh and that in itself can start a long conversation. The point is to not just flat out tell her she's looking good. You want to play with it and of course making her laugh is always something you want to do.

NOTE: I've used that line before and it worked so go ahead… try it.

What next!?

So if things are going good you need to stick it out until the end and see what happens.

First, if she doesn't want you to join her she'll let you know – and what are you going to do?

Yep you guessed it, get her digits. Get her number and tell her you'll call her – and you will. Getting numbers is always a priority as it sets up future chances of getting laid.

Let's say, which this is very common, she says, "What are you doing after ...(wherever you are)?_" This question comes up all the time and what I like to say is:

"I don't know. I thought I'd come home with you" and give a little smile to her.

This is when she's going to let you know if you are getting lucky or if you're settling for digits. If she smiles than you know you're in. I know it seems a little gutsy but trust me, something like that works far more than saying something like, "I don't know... what are you doing later?"

It looks like you two are going home with each other – now what?!

First, go to her place. You want her to be as comfortable as possible. The more comfortable she is the better. The only exception is if she says that you can't, because she'll mean it.

So you go home with her and get into her room.

Do not, I repeat – DO NOT GO TO THE BATHROOM right away!

I don't care if you're about to urinate on yourself, you need to make a move before that. As long as you make a solid move – which is looking into her eyes – and pulling her in and initiate the kissing process, you can go to the bathroom after that's been accomplished.

That first kiss is so important, so make it a good one.

You've made it this far... have fun!

Last Note

I've had a lot of fun writing this book to help you get laid more, but this information will not ever help you if you don't just try it out.

The absolute hardest thing to do is to get the ball rolling. You must not be afraid to talk to women – I've already told you why not, but you have to follow through and decide that you want to get laid more.

I've taught you how I've did it for years and I know it works; you just need to take it all in and start practicing. The more practice you get the better you get, AND the more confidence you build.

OH WAIT! Bonus!

Getting women to sleep with you is just the first step but you should also know what to do when you are in bed with her. You have to do your best if you hope for a second time or you are in a long term relationship.

Most guys think they know everything about sex but most of the time this is not the case. So, please take some time and read the following chapter on how to have great sex. Even if you know everything it will certainly be useful to refresh your mind...

How To Have Great Sex

The Recipe for Great Sex

Imagine for a moment that you're sitting in a movie theater watching a really great movie. You're really having fun! There's adventure, excitement, romance, and even a touch of danger. But best of all, there's an aire of mystery and unpredictability. You have no idea what will happen next! Emotions are stirring, your hearts pounding, and then . . . there's the grand finale! The perfect ending to a perfect adventure. You release completely with a deep sigh. You walk out of the theater totally satisfied and maybe even a little tired. After all, that was one heck of an exhilarating experience!

Now . . . imagine watching the same movie . . . twice a week . . . for the next 3 months.

What happens at the end of the three months? For most of us, that movie will no longer be fun. It won't be adventurous. The excitement won't be there any longer. And the unpredictability? Haah... what unpredictability? You're got the entire darned script memorized by now! Without even trying!

To re-experience the fun, excitement and intrigue of watching a great movie, you have to watch a new movie, with a new plot, and new twists. It has to be unpredictable so that, while you know that the end will leave you breathless, you don't quite know how or when it will reach the end. With a new movie, you are once again able to enjoy each moment as it unfolds before your eyes.

Great sex, in many ways, is similar to watching a great movie. And just like a great movie, to be able to enjoy sex again and again, it has to be unique. It has to have new twists and turns, and it has to be unpredictable. Because when it's predictable, you know exactly what will happen and exactly when it will happen. You're back to watching that same darned movie over and over again. It's predictable. It's just not fun anymore. In fact, it's downright boring.

So... the secret ingredient to having great sex is variety! If I am asked to explain great sex in just one word, that would be it - variety. In order to keep sex interesting and fun, the what, the how, the when, and the where have to keep changing. In other words, the techniques, the execution, the time and the place have to change. They don't all have to change at the same time. But there has to be at least one change.

You may be thinking to yourself "Man, that's a lot of pressure! How can I always add something new to sex?" Well, you don't always have to do something new. But when you do, you'll find lots of ideas in this book.

Let's go back to the movie example for a better explanation. If you watched a great movie one time, there is a good chance that you will be able to enjoy that same movie again if you saw it a few months later. You may not enjoy it as much as the first time around, but you'll come pretty close.

Similarly, if every now and then you end up having sex exactly the same way as you did a month ago, you'll still enjoy it a lot, as long as you don't do the same thing every single time. The great thing about having sex is that, unlike watching a movie, it's almost impossible to have sex in exactly the same way as you did previously. And after you finish reading this book, you'll have enough ideas to be able to create an Oscar-winning blockbuster almost every single time!

So, let's get to it!

The Differences Between Men and Women

In order for both you and your partner to enjoy the experience, it's important that you learn a little more about how the other person works. What works for you may not always work for your partner. If you're trying to row a boat and the two of you are peddling in different directions, it will get very frustrating, you won't enjoy the ride, and you'll never reach your destination.

So, let's learn a little about how you can satisfy your partner and how your partner can satisfy you, and make this ride a lot more interesting.

Men can usually be ready for sex immediately. And... the moment they're ready for sex, they're ready for intercourse. Most women usually need at least 15 minutes of foreplay before they are ready for intercourse. This isn't a habit or preference. It's just how their bodies work.

Since we are not born with this knowledge about the opposite sex, it is time we learn it. Trust me, it will serve you well!

The Assumptions

Since men are ready for intercourse right away, their immediate area of focus is their genitals. And, since they want to be touched and pleasured in their genital area immediately, they assume that this is also true for women. As a result, during foreplay, men are in a hurry to get to the woman's genitals. For men, this is the best way to give pleasure to the woman because this is how they would like to be pleasured.

In contrast, women need more time spent on foreplay before they are ready for intercourse. So, they assume this is true for men as well. And as a result, during foreplay, most women will touch a man everywhere but his genitals. Just like the man, the woman assumes that since this is how her body works, it is probably the best way to give pleasure to the man as well.

And so begins the dance of confusion where everyone's stepping on everyone else's toes. The man will want to touch and pleasure the woman in her genital area immediately or he will want to get to intercourse, which will make the woman feel rushed. The woman will touch the man everywhere else until the man finally grabs her hand and puts it on his genitals.

It's safe to say that the result of this experience is confusion and frustration. If the man gets his way and speeds through everything, the woman is left unsatisfied and sometimes sore. If the woman is able to slow things down so it works out better for her, the man may feel frustrated or even rejected. He may feel that he's doing something wrong.

It's a mess, to put it mildly.

So, how can we fix this?

Well, the fact that you're taking the time to read this book is a great start. The only way to fix the problem is through knowledge, as we've mentioned before.

What Men Should Know

The best advice I can give to men is to s l o w d o w n.

Men need to spend more time on kissing and touching her before they go anywhere near her genitals. (The actual techniques will be covered in more detail later.)

If needed, have a clock in the room as a guide. Of course, don't make it obvious that you're timing yourself. It's just an aid. The reason for this exercise is to illustrate that the time elapsed during sex usually seems much faster to the man than the actual time elapsed. While you're kissing her, it may seem to you that 5 minutes have passed when in fact it will usually be much less.

Here's a great comparison:

If a man and a woman were sitting across a table enjoying some ice cream, the man would usually be done with the ice cream very quickly. That's just how he eats. Some men will actually swallow it whole, if they could, within a few seconds.

Sitting across from him is the woman. The woman will usually take her time with the ice cream, or any other dessert for that matter. She will savor every moment, every molecule.

She will tease herself with it. She will make the pleasure last as long as she can. She will take a spoon of it and barely touch her tongue with it. She will close her eyes and feel that tiny drop of sweet, creamy ice-cream melt on her tongue. Ummmmm.... Heaven, thy name be Rocky Road.

That's a woman's idea of pleasure . . . Indulgence.

So, while there is a time and place for quickies, and I will definitely cover that later, for the most part, be the delectable dessert for her so you can both enjoy the experience for a much longer period of time.

What Women Should Know

In contrast, the advice we'd like to given women is to speed up just a little.

Start stimulating his genital area fairly quickly.

While you're both kissing and engaging in foreplay, you can provide pleasure to his genital area. When you do this, you will be giving him what he needs and there is a greater chance that he'll enjoy foreplay more, and for a longer period of time, since he's getting what he wants, for now. If he starts to progress too quickly, keep pleasuring him his way as you say to him "Let's enjoy this a little longer."

Men are fairly easy to please. They just need to be trained to not rush but instead enjoy every second of the experience.

Additional Notes

It's also helpful that both men and women discuss their likes, dislikes, and fantasies with each other, especially if you are in a serious relationship. Ask each other what turns them on and what their secret fantasies are. This does not have to be done during sex. It can be done any time you're alone with each other. Make mental notes of what you learn during this discussion.

Both of you should also try to stay in shape and keep looking attractive to each other. What I mean is, don't dress like a slob simply because you now have someone to have sex with. Don't stop exercising now that you're with someone. The longer you've been together, the more important this is. Physical attraction may not be high on your list if you've been together for a while, but it definitely will not hurt.

Regular exercise and healthy eating is good for you regardless. Exercise also increases libido and ensures that all your sex organs are functioning at optimal level. Studies have shown that regular exercise also helps men last longer in bed. In women, exercise has shown to improve their ability and frequency of achieving orgasms. Exercise is very important for having great sex. That's a great reason to hit the gym together. And afterwards, you could hit the showers together too. See how well that "works out?"

Care enough about the other person to find out what turns them on and what turns them off. Take mental notes, during sex, about their likes and dislikes related to sex. If you're doing something that turns the other person on, make a note of it and use it sometime in the near future. And if something doesn't seem to do too well, lose it.

If the man in the relationship is the one who initiates sex all or most of the time, the woman should work on being the initiator more often than she normally does. This also helps the woman to be more open and comfortable with sex. And it tells the man that she's just as excited about having sex with him and that he doesn't always have to be the pursuer.

It seems that many women, no matter how beautiful, feel insecure about how their body looks to her partner, especially during sex. They need to relax more during sex and not be concerned about what they "think" the guy is thinking about her body. That fact of the matter is that you're willingly there with them, and you're naked. At that moment, you are the best looking woman he has ever seen. Trust us on this one.

Foreplay
For most men, sex equals intercourse. For women, intercourse is just one part of sex, and they are correct.

Think of it this way, if you really wanted to see a great movie and were really looking forward to watching it, how would you feel if I came over to you and gave the ending away? Would that ruin the movie for you? You know it will. That is exactly how most women feel during sex. While they are thinking of enjoying every fulfilling minute of the movie, most men usually give the ending away and ruin it.

Not a good thing. Let's change that.

Men can usually be ready for sex immediately; they can get an erection quickly. Most women usually need at least 15 minutes of foreplay before they are ready. Without foreplay, a woman's vagina and clitoris do not get aroused enough and are not ready for direct stimulation.

Men need to realize that foreplay can be just as enjoyable for them, as it is for women, if they only take the time to try it.

To make the most of foreplay, it has to be fun. You have to be relaxed and be ready to make the most of it. While men are usually in a hurry to get to the end, they should remember to relax, take long deep breaths and learn to enjoy foreplay. The sex that will follow will be all that more intense and pleasurable.

While I don't want to discuss the mechanics of the techniques too much in this chapter, I will briefly elaborate on a few of them as needed. (We will get into the techniques in more detail in another chapter.)

I'd also like to point out at this time that "Kissing" can be one of the best and simplest forms of foreplay.

A great kiss from their lovers can also tell women that great sex is usually just around the corner.

As one woman put it, "If my partner wants to get me ready for sex, the best way to do it is with a long, slow, passionate kiss!"

Since the subject of kissing is a fairly important one, I will cover it in further detail in the next chapter.

Now, here are a few tips on making foreplay more fun and enjoyable:

Both partners should use their hands, fingertips, lips and tongue in as many ways as they can think of.

Keep the other person guessing.

Vary the pressure, speed, and strokes of your touches to add the sense of unpredictability. Instead of starting at the lips and moving straight down in a linear fashion, alternate. For example, if men usually start at the lips and then move to the neck, chest, tummy, and set up camp in the nether regions, they need to try a variation as follows: start at the lips, move on to the neck, then the chest, and up to the ears. Then move back to the lips, and then the tummy. Remember, if your partner can predict what your next move is, it will usually become boring.

Here's another suggestion: if you always start by kissing on the lips, let's change that. Next time, start by kissing your partners fingers and hands. Or start at the feet and work your way up. Keep it light, fun and unpredictable.

Experiment with different textures and temperatures. Use lotions, oils, silk scarves, feathers, ice cubes and so on, on each other's bodies. The keyword here is variety. Sex will never be boring as long as you're willing to be creative and open to new sensations.

Feed each other dessert. Try chocolate ice cream, water-rich fruits (strawberries, oranges, cantaloupe, etc.), or just whipped cream.

Or, instead of feeding each other, try eating or licking foods off each other's bodies.

Giving each other a sensuous massage is also very enjoyable form of foreplay.

The possibilities are endless. All you need is an open mind and a sense of adventure and fun! For more ideas, read the chapter on "Variety."

Tip for men: While 15 minutes is usually enough to get a woman ready for sex, don't let that limit you. I'm sure you can enjoy it for a much longer period. I have faith in you!

Extended Foreplay

While foreplay just before sex is always helpful for a more enjoyable experience, that is not the only time you can indulge in foreplay.

Foreplay doesn't have to start right before sex. It can start hours, and sometimes even days before the main event. It can start even when you're far away from each other. And boy are you going to love it!

All-day foreplay

Plan an entire day for just the two of you and plan to have sex at the very end of the day. Do your favorite things together: a picnic, hiking, shopping, enjoying a favorite sport or hobby, and so on. Touch and kiss each other a lot. Tease, seduce, whisper in their ears, talk dirty, and more. Do everything except have sex.

Tell each other how turned on they make you. Let each other know how eagerly you're awaiting and looking forward to the night. It may be difficult to last the whole day, but the rewards at the end will be well worth the wait. I should warn you: it may involve some clothes-ripping or property damage, or both.

Show a woman that she's lust worthy and she'll prove it to you! If you can sincerely, through your words and actions, let a woman know how much she turns you on, not only will this be the best foreplay she has experienced, she will also deliver sex beyond your wildest dreams.

Whisper in her ear while you're out in public, at a party or any other gathering or event. Tell her that you can't stop thinking about seeing her naked tonight. The key here is to drive each other crazy through your words and touch. When you do get to the sex, it will be all that more amazing. Women can also use these ideas on men.

Tell each other how crazy they drive you every time you look at them. Touch each other in ways that tell the person that you can't seem to keep your hands off of them. Make your partner feel sexy, attractive and desirable, and they will show you just how wild they can get in bed.

Women can do the same to men. Whisper in his ear and tell him what exactly you plan to do to him when you two are alone. Get as graphic as you need to be to get the point across. Remember, men are visual. The right words will get them visualizing in advance!

Indulge in foreplay and turn each other on at night just before bedtime, and when you're both at the brink of climaxing, stop and call it a night. That's right, we're saying stop before you're both about to reach orgasm and say good night. Arrange this ahead of time so you both know what the plan is. When you wake up the next morning, continue from where you left off. We're not saying that this will be easy to do, but... if you can survive the night, the sex that morning will be unforgettable.

The Kiss
To most guys, a kiss is a way to get to sex. And for this reason, they usually don't spend much time on it. To many women, a kiss is everything! To some, it is also the best form of foreplay. And since most women need foreplay before they can get ready for sex, spending time kissing is very, very important.

Forget the movies and take it slow. While a passion-filled, furniture demolishing, clothe-ripping kiss is great on occasion, try the slow motion version for most kisses. You have a much better chance of achieving mutual satisfaction.

Use this as a guideline: Spend at least 5 minutes on kissing before any clothes are taken off.

Here are a few tips on making you a much better kisser:
A kiss has to start out slow, and very soft. Don't immediately involve the tongue into the kiss.

Start by letting each others lips touch very softly and gently, almost to a point where you can't really tell whether you've started to kiss or not. Very slowly increase the intensity, using light strokes and gentle nibbles.

Another great way to start is by softly and slowly circling the outside of the other person's lips with your tongue, or the tip of your finger.

And then start the actual kiss.

When your tongues do finally touch, it's still done softly and erotically. Let your tongue play with the other person's tongue.

Men can gently suck on the woman's lower lip while kissing.

Enjoy the kissing. Don't worry about what's coming next.

Give each other a chance to kiss you back too. And enjoy how that feels. Take turns leading while the other receives. Then let the other person lead while you receive.

A good tip for men is to hold her face with your hands lightly when you first kiss her. Women love that! It's warm, romantic, and sexy all at the same time.

Men can also lift her up by the waist occasionally during the kiss. This makes her feel slim, and sexy, and very feminine.

Use your fingertips to slowly trace each other's faces and neck. Many find this very romantic and sensual.

Spend at least 30 seconds kissing on the lips before moving to the ears or her neck. And then, be sure to come back to the lips again. Remember . . . be a little unpredictable.

This may sound obvious but is often forgotten or ignored. Men should kiss a lot more during intercourse, not just before and after. And definitely kiss her just as she's about to have an orgasm. It will take her breath away.

Variety
Far from Ordinary Sex

As you are already aware of, if you use the same positions, techniques, and surroundings for sex every time, the sizzle dies away. It's not fun anymore. There's no sense of adventure and intrigue. It's predictable and therefore boring. You may be able to enjoy it the first few times, but after that, it doesn't have the same effect of excitement and passion anymore. You know exactly what's going to happen next. You've heard the joke before. You know the punch line. It's time for a new one.

Variety is what takes ordinary sex and turns it into extraordinary sex! It's turns boring and tedious sex into a fun and intriguing, wild adventure.

And remember . . . variety does not just mean trying all the different things that you know of at different times, it also means trying new things that you have not tried before. It means being open to adventure and new experiences, as long as it is mutually agreeable.

Keep in mind that if you're planning on trying out something very kinky or outrageous, it is advisable that you discuss them with your partner in advance so there are no surprises or uncomfortable moments. This will also show that you respect the other person. Mutual agreement is very important.

With that little insight out of the way, here are a few suggestions to spice up your sex life:

It Just Makes Sense

You have five wonderful and powerful senses at your disposal: touch, sight, smell, taste, and hearing. Why not use them all!

The most obvious one for most of us is the sense of touch. You may already be familiar with the use of your hands, palms, fingers, fingertips, lips, and tongue. You may also be using your feet, toes, rubbing limbs against limbs, etc.

Here are a few more suggestions that you may or may not know of to get all your senses involved:

Experiment with different textures, temperatures, and pressures. Vary the intensity, speed, and stroke of your touches to fully activate the senses.

Use silk scarves, feathers, ice cubes and such on each other's bodies. Some people have even experimented with hot candle wax and enjoyed it. You can decide for yourself if that's for you. The key here is variety. Sex will never be boring as long as you're willing to be creative and open to new sensations and adventures.

Give each other a sensuous massage using lotions or scented oils. This will activate the sense of touch and smell. Take your time and cover every inch of the body.

You could also use your tongue to lick something edible off your partner's body.

Try using chocolate and/or whipped cream. Feed each other or feed off of each other's bodies, and of course, use your tongue to clean up afterwards.

There also a lot of toys and novelty items

available for adventurous couples that can provide new sensations and great vibrations. Visit your neighborhood adult novelty store or check out the Internet.

Wear sexy and revealing clothes, underwear, and/or lingerie to appeal to the sense of sight.

And of course, we've heard that the birthday suit also works very well, but we prefer it if something is left to the imagination.

How about doing a striptease for your lover, or watching an erotic movie together.

Turn of all the lights and use only candles. The candlelight as well as the shadows it casts on the walls from the activities in the room will definitely appeal to the senses.

Use incense, scented oils, and lotions. Wear the perfume/cologne that your partner loves the most. Use any scents. You can even combine this with the previous suggestion and use scented candles.

You can also use fresh flowers and/or rose petals on the bed or in a bath.

Feed each other a favorite dessert. Try chocolate ice cream, water-rich fruits (strawberries, oranges, cantaloupe, etc.), or just plain whipped cream.

Use music to set the right mood: romantic, sexy, wild, sensuous, etc.

Also experiment with theme sounds such as sounds of nature, wilderness, jungle, tropical, waterfall, etc.

Read seductive poetry or share an erotic story together.

Talk dirty to each other. Tell the other person what you'd like to do to them. (Start out slow when talking dirty or discuss the likes, dislikes and limits of it in advance. It is not for everyone.)

Try phone sex with each other, or simply describe what you would do during sex, from start to finish.

Many people are also turned on by the sounds their partners make during sex. You can also add to the moanings things like "That feels so great; You look so wonderful, beautiful, sexy; You taste/smell so good" etc. Some people like talking this way during sex.

Again, you are only limited by your own imagination. The possibilities are endless. Sex does not have to be boring, ever again!

What, When, Where, and How
Activities

Watch a scary movie together. Studies show that people, especially women, tend to mistake the feelings of fear with that of being aroused. Well, we can use this! After watching a scary flick together, don't let that arousal factor go to waste. You may even want to create your own movie. For private screening only, of course.

Watch an adult movie together. Yes, we know that women are not supposed to enjoy this as much as the guys. The next time you watch an adult movie "together", notice how many positions you can pick up on. Try out the tasteful ones. Of course, if you have to watch it alone, then so be it. Be sure to take notes.

And to balance it out, you may now have to also try watching a romantic movie together. Yes, I hear the guys booing in the back. Just try it anyway. And while you're watching, hold hands, be in each other's arms, maybe even kiss occasionally, or heck, maybe even a little touching and fondling. But no heavy stuff till the movie is over. And then, pull out all the stops.

Exercise together. Exercise tends to not only increase your stamina but it also increases your libido. And it helps all your systems function better, including the sexual ones. That means longer, more enjoyable sex. What more reason do you need?

Play a sport or game together that involves a lot of touching and holding. How about a game of naked Twister?

Take showers together. Can this also help save on water? Yes. But the important question here is... whose turn is it to pick the soap up from the floor?

Take a hot shower or bath together. Slowly and erotically lather each other up. Spend additional time on the erogenous zones: chest/breasts, buttocks, stomach, back, back of neck, inner thighs, etc.

Offer to wash her hair and give her a scalp massage. Ooops, someone just dropped the soap... ahem... by accident. Come on, one of you has to get on your knees. And while you're down there, you could actually try looking for that soap, if you're into that sort of thing.

Read sexy bedtime stories together.

If you can't find any, ask her to share one

of her romance novels. If she doesn't have any, just step into any major bookstore and you'll find an entire row full of these novels. They vary from light romance to hard-core porn. Take your pick. Talk dirty to each other. Start slow and see what works for the two of you.

Enjoy mutual masturbation. You will also get to learn more about how to please your partner more during sex. And it will bring you closer to each other.

Take afternoon naps on weekends. Whoever wakes up first can wake the other up with oral sex. Talk about this and discuss the idea ahead of time so there is no surprise or weirdness to it. It may not be for everyone.

If that's too much for one of you, stick to massage or slow, soft fondling using hands and/or tongue. Wake each other up this way instead.

Dance can be a great foreplay. Being close to each other, breathing, light touching, combined with the aroma of colognes and/or perfumes can do just the trick. Dirty dancing anyone?

Dance in your underwear. No, not the ones you wear on laundry day. Try something sexy and erotic. Something along the lines of Victoria's Secret and International Male.

Play strip poker or any other games that you can attach the word "strip" to. There are no losers in this game.

Take a "quickie" break while out hiking. Camping can be a lot of fun too - Be sure to pack a sturdy tent. Being around nature somehow gets people thinking about sex. See if it brings out the animal in you!

Timing Makes Champions

Think your lives are too busy for sex? Think again.

Here are a few tips to overcome the 'time' challenge and a few added bonuses:

Call your lover out of the blue and schedule a "lunch" date. In fact, skip lunch and just go straight for dessert. Is that what they call a "nooner?"

Wake up an hour to 1/2 hour earlier in the morning. Sex hormones peak in the mornings for both men and women. What better time to have sweaty, steamy, passionate sex?

If you still have the energy, hit the showers together afterwards. Sex in showers is not just for mornings though. It can be good anytime.

Get to bed 1/2 hour earlier than usual. Hmm, what could we do with the extra 1/2 hour? No, watching TV is not what I had in mind, unless it involves steamy scenes.

How about a midnight snack? Make plans to wake up in the middle of the night and play chess. Or you could just have incredible sex instead. Your choice.

Of course, whomever wakes up first can enjoy waking the other one up using hands and tongue only.

Get creative. Think of all the things you do during your day and how you could do those things together. Showers and lunches are just the beginning.

Never again will you say, "I don't have time for sex."

Location, Location, Location

Again, building on the fact that change kills boredom, start by setting a clear rule:

As often as you can, you are to have sex anywhere but the bedroom.

That simple rule can open you up to a lot of creative alternatives: couch, coffee table, bath tub, the shower, kitchen, kitchen table, rocking chair, exercise equipment, standing against a wall or laying on the floor of every room in the house. And that's just "inside the house."

How about the backyard, the garage, in the car, hood of the car, out in the woods during camping or hiking or picnicking.

Any public place can spice things up for that matter. Having sex where there's a probable danger of being caught adds a unique spark and excitement to sex. Try the swimming pool, the host's bedroom at a party, sneaking away after dinner at your parents, a stairwell, at work in your office (or an empty office or even your boss's office!) Some have also tried the airplane restroom. But do all of this at your own risk. If you get caught, don't blame me.

You could also rent a motel room, or even a romantic hotel package.

Take a cruise together; rent a cabin or timeshare in another city, state, or country.

I have provided a lot of suggestions to start you up.

However, anything that changes the scenery and breaks the monotony will work! Imagine that you're teenagers having sex for the very first time. All you need to do is spend a little time, put a little effort into thinking of new things and places to use. Your brain will provide the rest.

Some people also find it fun to delve into the fantasy world. Go out to a bar and meet each other as if you're on a first date. Or try picking each other up as if you've just met for the very first time. It will be fun for others watching too. Just don't leave the bar with someone else unless you want to check in to good ol' Fido's place for the night.

Technique

Improving your technique does not just mean learning the mechanics of new moves, it also means being flexible enough to adapt moves you already know to different situations, moods, and moments.

The basic idea, again, is to kill the boredom, to stay as far away from "ordinary" as you can. Your goal is to be extraordinary! Remember, the keyword is variety.

As I mentioned earlier, if you use the same positions, techniques and places for sex every time, the sizzle dies away. There's no sense of adventure or intrigue. It's predictable. It's boring. It's just not fun.

Also, as stated earlier, men can usually be ready for intercourse immediately. Many women usually need at least 15 minutes of foreplay before they are ready. It's just how the male and female bodies are different. Accept it, and learn to work with it.

As we started to discuss in an earlier

chapter, men and women are different.

Generally, men go straight for the woman's genitals, because that's what they would want to be done to them. They are ready now! And they assume that women function the same way. Women usually go along with it. They don't usually give verbal or physiological feedback to correct the mistake - probably to save the male ego. After all, most men think they know how to please women.

Women, on the other hand, don't go straight for the man's genitals. In fact, they will touch him everywhere else but the genitals until the man finally takes her hand and puts it on his genitals. She's touching and kissing him the way that feels good to "her" - the way that she would like to be touched. She assumes what feels good to her will feel good to him.

So . . . How can we correct this?

For Men

Men need to slow down. Touch her everywhere but her vagina and/or clitoris, at least for the first 5 to 15 minutes. Females have erogenous zones and hot spots all over the body.

Hit them all, and enjoy them all. The female body is a work of art. If she's taken the time to show you all, appreciate all of it.

To really drive her crazy, when you do get to the genital area, instead of touching directly on the vagina or clitoris, tease her. Touch her all around the vaginal opening, the area under the vagina, the inner thighs, etc. When she absolutely cannot stand it any longer, slowly touch the main areas. Using this teasing technique, you may sometimes be able get her to climax with the first few touches since the intensity has been built up so much.

Here's another way of looking at it...

Notice how men eat ice cream. They will usually be done within a blink of an eye. Now, watch women eat ice cream. Most of them will take their time, and savor every moment, and every molecule. They will tease themselves with it, place it in their mouths, close their eyes and be lost in heaven as it melts on the tip of the tongue. Ummm . . .

That's their idea of pleasure. So, while quickies and nooners have their place, in most cases be the dessert for them that they can enjoy for longer periods of time.

You may be asking yourself "Why should I do all this for her?" Well, for one, you're reading this book to become better in bed. Correct? Good. If you still need a reason, here's one good one: If you can fully satisfy a woman and really give her pleasure in bed, she will give you pleasure 10-fold, in return! Good enough for ya?

Let's continue...

Most men start by kissing on the lips, then move to the neck, the breasts, the stomach, and raise camp when they get to the end zone.

It's predictable. She knows exactly what you're going to do next, every time you play the same movie again. She knows you're going to start at her lips and head straight down in a straight line, kissing once or twice in between. That is the quickest road to boredom. Since erogenous zones are present all over the body, hit them all and alternate them. Use different strokes, rhythms, speeds, keep her guessing. Zig where you would normally zag.

Here's a quick example of what you could do:

While you're kissing her on the lips, slowly brush your hand on her crotch while her panties are still on. As you're doing this, move from kissing her lips to her neck, and then her breasts. Then, throw her off, and go back to her lips. Then down to her tummy. Brush your lips over her pubic hair ever so slowly. Then, back up to her breasts.

The mystery and unpredictability will drive her nuts! It will turn her on and when you do get to her vagina, it will be that much more pleasurable for her, and for you!

The next time, try a variation of the above. Add something new; omit something that was done before. Try new positions, different thrust speeds and angles, try new places - forget the bed. Try the recliner or the couch.

Sometimes, a new technique can simply be to use a previous technique in a different theme or context.

Direct stimulation
When you're using your hands or tongue to stimulate her clitoris, don't make direct contact with the clitoris right away. Instead gently rub the hood and folds of the clitoris for a minute. Then, slowly expose the head and gently move your finger/tongue in circles around the clitoris.

As you notice her getting closer to orgasm, start rubbing against the clitoris directly, but be very gentle. Also be sure that there is adequate lubrication or it will be painful for her. When she begins to orgasm, switch back to stimulating around the clitoris instead of direct stimulation. During her orgasm, the clitoris will become highly sensitive and direct contact can be painful.

Multiple orgasms
The best way give her multiple orgasms is to slow down after she climaxes. No direct contact to the clitoris. Give her a few moments to catch her breath, and then start building her up again by using semi-direct contact/stimulation of the clitoris. Usually, she will be able to have another orgasm within the next 2 to 5 minutes.

To really take her breath away, kiss her with your lips as she orgasms.

For Women
Women can in turn speed up just a little. You can touch and kiss him on the chest, neck, tummy, and sides for a bit and then bring the penis into play. While you're kissing, you can rub against his crotch from the outside of his pants. Men usually enjoy a little more pressure than women do during the rubbing and fondling. Then, slide your hand inside his pants and do the same. Move on to stroking the penis with your hand. Gently rub against and fondle the scrotum. Don't worry, it won't break, as long as you're gentle. You can even squeeze them a little, but not too hard. The goal here is to prolong foreplay for you

while you're giving the man what he wants.

Since men need direct contact immediately, this will keep him happy while you're on your way to getting fully aroused.

Churning
When you're stimulating the penis, add this step for additional pleasure. While stroking the penis, use your other hand to gently hold the scrotum. Then, as you continue to stroke the penis, slowly and gently massage the scrotum with the other hand. He will love it.

The Milking Technique
Just as the man is about to have an orgasm, squeeze his penis. This usually intensifies the orgasms. If you're using your hand, squeeze around the penis while stroking. During intercourse, squeeze your vaginal walls to create the same effect. This technique works best when the woman is on top since it's easier for her to squeeze.

Modified Woman on Top
In the standard 'woman on top' position, the man lays on his back while the woman sits upright, on top of him. The woman has more control of the angle and speed of the thrusts and can therefore reach orgasm more easily. For the man, laying on his back usually delays ejaculation. So, it works well for both partners.

The modified version of this position helps both partners more. Instead of sitting upright, the woman can lean forward anywhere between a 45-degree to 60-degree angle, and use her hands for support. Then, instead of moving up and down, she moves her hips back and forth. This position allows for more clitoral stimulation for the woman and further helps the man to last longer when compared to the up and down motion.

While the woman is on top, she can use her hair to brush against the man's chest for his added pleasure.

Women can also work with their male partners and teach them to slow down and even last longer. Some tips are given later on in this chapter.

One final, yet important advice for women: The best way to get your partner to enjoy sex more is to simply have more sex. It helps to repeat the advice that women need to initiate sex more! This one step alone will improve your sex life dramatically.

Learn from Each Other
Just as you can satisfy each other by simply reversing the things you used to do to each other, you can similarly learn more about how to satisfy each other in different areas. By this type of sharing and interest in your partner, you can become better lovers for each other.

Show each other what your idea of the perfect kiss is. Take turns kissing each other but the other person cannot kiss back and just enjoys your kiss. Then switch. This will show you exactly how the other person likes to be kissed which you can then imitate.

Masturbate in front of each other while

the other person watches - and takes mental notes. The observer can also join in by some basic touching or kissing eventually. This will help you, and your lover, learn a whole lot about satisfying each other.

Some people may find this technique to be uncomfortable at first. But work through it because doing so will also bring the two of you closer and more intimate. This in turn will increase the enjoyment and pleasure during sex.

Try to get each other to orgasm without intercourse. Use only your hands and lips and tongue. Or, use only your hands today. And tomorrow, use only your lips and tongue.

The person being satisfied can provide feedback verbally or physically, as needed.

Last Longer in Bed

One of the most frequent complaints, from both men and women, is that men tend to reach orgasms much faster then women. The bad news is you may be one of these men.

The good news that it's a fairly common problem. You're not the only one. The really great news is that the problem can be fixed.

Here are two simple techniques men can use to increase their lasting time:

1. Build and Stop

This technique requires the man to stroke his penis with his hand until he feels he is close to reaching orgasm. Then, stop stroking, take a deep breath in, and then slowly breathe out. Repeat the breathing until the urge to climax surpasses.

Then, repeat the process.

This process will help the man to gain better control of his orgasms.

When he is able to control his orgasms, the next step is to try the same technique using lubrication. The goal here is to duplicate the sensations of actual intercourse. This process will be more difficult than the one above.

When he is able to control orgasms using lubrication, he can then graduate to using this technique during actual intercourse. With practice, men have been able to last as long as they want during sex by delaying their orgasms using this 'build and stop' technique.

2. Kegel Exercises

Doing Kegel exercises is another way to delay ejaculation and last longer during sex. It is done by contracting and relaxing your PC muscles. To locate your PC muscles, try moving your penis without using your hands. The muscles used to do this are your PC muscles. They are also the muscles you use to stop yourself from urinating. These muscles, on an average guy, is usually not strong enough to stop ejaculation.

However, just as is true for any other muscle, by exercising them, they can become stronger and help you to control your ejaculations.

Simply contract these muscles, hold for a second, and relax them. And then repeat the process. Start by doing 50 repetitions per session and build up to as many as you can do without feeling any pain. You can do these anywhere, even while you're sitting in the car waiting for the light to change or sitting in your office surfing the net. No one will know.

You can do them once or twice per day, every day. If you feel any discomfort or pain the next day, take a break and continue the following day. Just as with any other exercise, start slow and don't over do it.

Most men see improvements within 1 to 3 months. After the first 3 months, it may not be necessary to do Kegels every day. However, to maintain the strength, continue to exercise the PC muscles occasionally. If you can handle doing it everyday, that's great.

Now it's time to put your stronger PC muscles to the test...

As you feel yourself reaching closer to orgasm, clamp your PC muscles by contracting them as hard as you can. Hold for up to 1 minute or until the urge to ejaculate surpasses and then slowly relax the muscles. As you relax, let a long deep breath out. Repeat this process for as long as you need to.

Strong PC muscles can practically help you last as long as you want in bed. When you do finally allow yourself to ejaculate, the ejaculation will be much stronger and the orgasms more intense.

Move over, Viagra!

Positions

If you start with the missionary position and end with the missionary each time, it's time to get creative.

While there are many different positions to share, I will cover some of the best ones that I feel will improve the quality of sex for both partners as well as help solve the most common problems/complaints among couples.

The positions we discuss will:

• ensure that women have more frequent orgasms during sex

• help men last longer

• solve the "penis size" problem, and of course

• offer enough variety to kill boredom

And the nominees are . . .

A Position That Almost Guarantees Orgasms for Both

This is called the modified missionary position. While in the missionary position, the male will move his body up by one or two inches without pulling out of the female. While in this position, he will use only his hands and elbows to move up and down instead of moving his hips to penetrate in and out. This position will allow the man to last longer and it will also provide more stimulation to the woman's clitoris. The chances of both parties having orgasms is increased exponentially. There's also a good chance of simultaneous orgasms.

Modified Woman on Top

While this one is covered in a previous chapter, I felt it was worth repeating here.

In the standard 'woman on top' position, the man lays on his back while the woman sits upright, on top of him. The woman has more control of the angle and speed of the thrusts and can therefore reach orgasm more easily. For the man, laying on his back usually delays ejaculation. So, it works well for both partners.

The modified version of this position helps both partners more. Instead of sitting upright, the woman can lean forward anywhere between a 45-degree to 60-degree angle, and use her hands for support. Then, instead of moving up and down, she moves her hips back and forth. This position allows for more clitoral stimulation for the woman and further allows the man to last longer when compared to the up and down motion.

Sideways

Both the man and woman lie on their sides, facing each other. They can both bend their top legs (the legs that are furthest from the ground) at the knees, the man keeping his leg between the woman's legs while the woman rest her upper leg over the man's waist. The woman can rest her head on the man's lower arm (the arm closer to the ground.) This position also allows men to last longer while providing women with greater stimulation/friction. Also, neither one of the people involved has to support the other's body weight on top of their own. Both partners can rest on their sides.

If Size Matters . . .
Deeper Penetration
The female is laying on the table (or bed) on her back, using only her upper body so that her butt rests on the edge of the table. Her lower body is vertical, legs fully extended and toes pointing towards the ceiling. The man enters her while allowing her to rest her legs on his shoulders, one on each side. This position allows for deeper penetration.

A Variation of the Above
The female lays in bed on her back while her legs are vertical, fully extended. The male is sitting upright, legs folded, one knee resting on each side of the woman's body. She lifts her legs up and puts them on each side of his shoulders. The male can gently hold on to her legs for stability as he moves his hips back and forth. This position also allows for deeper penetration.

More Friction
This is a variation of the previous two positions. The difference is that instead of the woman resting her legs on each side of the man's shoulders, she rest both legs on just one of his shoulders and then she places one knee over the other so that her ankles are crossed. This allows both her thighs to press against each other creating a narrower opening in her vagina which in turn creates more friction during penetration. Both partners will feel more friction and more stimulation during

intercourse. Be certain that there is adequate lubrication.

Doggie Style
The female assumes the kneeling position, resting on her knees and elbows. Her upper arms are extended in front of her on which she can rest her head. The male, resting on his knees, enters her from behind. This position also allows for more penetration.

Variation of Above Position
This is a variation of the doggie style. The female lays on her tummy on a bed or table while her legs are hanging from the edge of the bed/table. The male is standing, and enters from behind, again allowing for greater penetration.

Caution: Keep in mind that greater penetration is not always better. If the penetration is too deep, it can cause the woman pain and can sometimes also cause internal damage.

Use good judgment.

An Added Tip Regarding Size
Some experts suggest that when a woman is fully aroused before penetration, her vaginal opening appears to decrease in size and also creates a suction mechanism around the penis. This can compensate for a not-so-large penis.

So, the best thing guys can do is to enjoy lots of foreplay before intercourse, if size is an issue!

Other Positions for Variety

Try having sex standing up. The woman can lean against the wall. The man lifts one of her legs up and enters her. This is not an easy position and may require some practice. If the man is taller than the woman is, he may have to stand with his feet spread further apart to compensate for the height difference.

Try different positions in the tub. This can be a lot of fun. Although, be careful of slipping accidents.

Don't let this limit your imagination. Using different "places", for example, the recliner instead of the couch, will give you a chance to find new and more interesting positions for both you and your partner.

Generally, women prefer that you don't break contact once you're inside her. So, unless you're changing to another position that requires you to pull out of her first, stay inside her for as long as you can.

While we're on the subject, here's another way to make things more exciting:

Start with one position, and change to up to 5 other positions without breaking contact, i.e. without pulling out. Let's see how creative you can get. Take your time with this one. Don't rush during the changes and don't pull any muscles. You don't want to injure yourself or your partner.

Quickies

The most important thing you should keep in mind is that quickies are not meant to be an alternative to regular sex. They should not replace regular sex. A quickie is an added spice you can sprinkle on to your existing incredible sex lives to make it even more exciting.

Quickies, if done right can be good for both partners! Here's how you can make them a lot more fun:

Quickies seem to be a lot more fun when they're unplanned and spontaneous. This usually catches the other person off guard. It's not predictable and that is a "good thing."

It also tells the other person that you desire them and are very attracted to them, that you can't control your lust for them and that you have to have them now! It may also help to verbally convey these things to your partner. Everyone wants to feel desired.

Quickies need to be passionate, maybe even a little rough. Imagine the sound of clothes being ripped off, while kissing passionately and hurriedly. Imagine one of you pushing the other down towards the bed or sofa. It's like going from zero to 60 in 5 seconds!

The spontaneity and raw passion involved in quickies can usually get women aroused and ready for intercourse just as quickly as men. They may even have an orgasm during quickies if the right ingredients are present. This is one of those rare cases where foreplay is not required. Besides, there's no time for it. Hence the name "quickie."

However, if she doesn't seem to have enjoyed it as much as the man, the man should promise to make it up to her at a later time. And he should definitely keep his promise!

And when he does, he should make it all

about her. Give her oral pleasure and make the whole thing last for as long as you can, without expecting anything in return. Of course, if she insists on repaying the favor immediately, who are we to stop her?

Quickies are also great when done spontaneously, in an "unfamiliar environment," i.e. not in your own bed, and hopefully not on a bed at all.

Also, as mentioned earlier, a little danger of being caught somehow enhances the pleasure. Some examples: in a public place, in a not-so-secluded parking lot, sneaking away to an empty room while at a party, under a stairwell, etc. Of course, if you get caught, I am not sending you bail money.

Think back to what sex was like as a teenager. Do you recall wanting to have sex every chance you got, at every place you could find that could offer you just 5 minutes of privacy? That's the kind of lust and passion that makes quickies satisfying.

And, lastly, as I mentioned before, quickies are not meant to be an alternative to regular sex. It should instead enhance your already existing, incredible sex life.

Aftermath

This section is mostly for men.

If you're in a serious relationship, and the other person means something to you, there may be a few things you would want to do (or not do) after you've had sex with her:

Don't roll over and fall asleep.

Don't get up immediately after you're done and walk out of the room either.

Most women actually prefer it if you spent a little time with her afterwards, holding her in your arms while you lay down together. Yeah, I know it probably sounds mushy to you. But it won't kill you to do so, and it will probably score you some major points because women love this stuff!

You could also stay inside her, after you've had sex, while you cuddle or lay next to each other. If you're using a condom, be careful with this one. There is a chance that the condom could slip out of your penis and get lodged inside her vagina.

The next time you have sex, think of how you could make it more fun, more romantic, more passionate and exciting for both you and your lover.

The tips provided in this book are just the beginning!

Appendix

Here are some great additional tips from my friend John Alexander. John is a well known pick up artist and the author of "How to Become an Alpha Male".

To find more about John and his techniques please visit:

www.foreverlaid.com/alfamale

Body Language

An estimated 67% to 93% of human communication (according to university researchers) is non-verbal, and your body language reveals your internal emotional state. Whether someone's parents just died, or whether they just got promoted to CEO... you can tell by observing their body language.

So, as a man who tries to pick up and seduce women, you should be mindful of what you're communicating non-verbally.

Body language consists of the following:

- Your movements. They should be nonchalant, as if you're so fabulously successful that there's rarely a reason for you to rush nor try to impress anybody. Move through the world doing what you want and assuming that others will follow.
- The displacement of your body. Your arms and legs should be spread out. Don't be afraid to take up space.
- Your voice. It should have a calm, soothing, and commanding effect. Don't speak too fast or strain your voice.
- Your face. Keep your facial muscles relaxed. Never tense your jaw, and only rarely should you frown or wrinkle your brow.
- Your shoulders. Keep them relaxed like they'd be if you just got a massage. Don't raise them up like a nervous person.

I would even go as far as to say that you body language is more important than anything you say, because if your body language doesn't match what you say, then you won't succeed with women.

You see, if you tell a woman stories that convey your confidence, but at the same time you slump over and fold your arms, then you come across as fake.

I've picked up women before merely through the use of my body language. For example, a couple months ago I was at a coffee shop that I frequent, lounging on the couch, arms spread out, with my feet up on the table.

The mindset I had was that I felt so comfortable that it was as if I were in my home lounging on my own couch. It was as if I owned the coffee shop.

The net result was that a girl sitting near me put down her book and started engaging me in random small talk.

(Whenever an attractive girl you don't know starts a random conversation with you, you should ALWAYS assume that she's attracted to you. This is because women generally won't risk the whole male-female dynamic, especially with a stranger, unless they feel attraction.)

The conversation went on for awhile, I got her number, called her that night, and a few days later we met and after several hours went to her place, where I spent the night. (We finally had sex in the morning.)

The bottom line though is that she became initially attracted to me and approached me because of my body language.

Now, of course body language isn't enough. You also must have an internal alpha male mindset that's consistent with your body language.

But make no mistake about it... if your body language conveys confidence, then your mood will also shift to become more confident. And have you ever noticed how when you walk with a spring in your step, you feel more upbeat?

Conversely, when you cast your eyes down and drag your feet, you feel depressed. So your mindset also follows the body language that you adopt.

So, in conclusion, be an alpha male with your mindset and your body language. Be in a woman's personal space and be sexual and interested in her, but at the same time don't be needy or desperate for her attention. Just be comfortable and enjoy yourself.

And when your body language conveys that, it means you'll later be comfortable and enjoying yourself... with the woman.

Use The Boyfriending Technique To Get Laid Fast

I'm going to reveal an important comfort-building technique I call "Boyfriending." In a nutshell, there's something you can do that's usually done ONLY by a woman's boyfriend.

If you do it too, it's a way of getting under a woman's radar and making her comfortable enough around you so that she'll be receptive to sex without making you wait.

You see, in order for a typical woman to have sex with a man, she must have feelings of comfort. It is not enough for her to simply feel attraction for the guy.

Let's say you meet a girl at a 5 PM happy hour. The two of you hit it off, having a great conversation. She's laughing. She's interested. You entrance her by telling her fascinating stories about your life. The two of you have good rapport. Around 7:30, you get hungry and invite her to get something to eat. Dinner goes well too. Then dinner ends. Now what?

Around this time, a lot of guys get confused about how to advance the interaction forward. Clearly the goal is to get laid, but the roadmap is often muddled.

Usually the night ends with the woman saying something like, "I had great time meeting you. Call me. Bye!"

Often, the need for comfort is why women like to make guys wait before sex.

(If the guy's lucky, it might be only three dates, but with a lot of women, the guy can be made to wait for months.)

Fortunately, there's a way to short circuit that barrier. I call it the "Boyfriending Technique."

If you watch couples who are in close relationships, you'll notice an interesting phenomenon. The man and woman are extremely comfortable touching each other, so much so that they'll even do seemingly gross things like brush sleep ("eye boogers") out of each other's eyes.

It's a behavior that's only done by people who are completely comfortable around each other. Certainly when you are in a relationship where you can brush sleep out of a woman's eye, you've long since passed the point where the two of you are comfortable having sex.

Catch my drift? You can use this as a psychological weapon to make the woman feel more comfortable around you.

In mid-conversation, tell her to hold still and close her eyes. Pretend there's sleep in her eye, and make her believe that you just brushed it off.

Later, after the two of you finish eating and leave the restaurant, again tell her to hold still. With your finger, brush off an imaginary piece of food from her lower lip.

The net result of the Boyfriending Technique is nuclear. First, it sub-communicates that the two of you are very comfortable around each other.

Second, it involves you touching her face, bringing your heads closer together and progressing towards a make out session.

Third, in the case of you touching her lower lip, you're in fact touching an erogenous zone. That's right... a woman's lower lip has a high concentration of nerve endings. Stimulating her lower lip makes her body release sex hormones.

Make the Boyfriending Technique a part of your dating arsenal, and you'll find more success than ever before. You may just be having sex within several hours instead of having to wait several months.

Using The Fated Encounter For First Date Seduction Success

Wouldn't it be nice if you could create feelings within a woman of a deep connection with you... even if you two have known each other for only a few hours... and without having to resort to complicated (and risky!) hypnosis tactics?

Well, good news. There is a very easy, no-risk way to do this. I call it the Fated Encounter Technique.

Here's why it works. Every woman has a fantasy from the time she was a little girl, triggered by a constant diet of romance movies and novels, about fate bringing the man of her dreams to her.

In one typical scene the guy and the girl almost bump into each other on the sidewalk. Instead, fate keeps them apart, and they go their separate ways.

Then, two years later, they live in the same apartment building. Yet after several close calls, they still don't meet, again because of fate.

The two date other people, off and on, and yet are never happy. Months go by. The man and the woman each ponder what it will be like when they meet that special someone, someday...

And then near the end of the movie, fate finally brings them together. And of course they hit it off right from the start.

Wouldn't it be nice if that could happen in real life, rather than having to wait through several dates before the woman finally feels comfortable enough with you to have sex?

Well, it can. You can speed the seduction process and have the woman feeling deeply connected with you by using my Fated Encounter Technique. I'll explain how it works.

During the course of your conversation with the woman, you bring up places she has been to. If you've been to those same places, you then talk about how amazing it is that the two of you could have been there at the same time and yet destiny kept you apart.

Let's say, to use a recent example I encountered, that she shops at the local Whole Foods grocery store.

You can then say, "That's awesome. I shop there too. Imagine, we've probably seen each other there all the time!"

Another example would be that the two of you go to downtown LA all the time, and probably have walked past each other on many occasions.

And now, you can say, "Isn't it amazing how fate has finally brought us together?"

As the conversation progresses, the two of you can talk about other coincidences, and the things the two of you might have done together if you'd only known each other.

With the seed planted, as the girl thinks about those coincidences, and how "fate" has now brought the two of you together, she will then start to feel as if she's known you, on a deeper psychic level, for a lot longer than just a few hours.

You, she concludes, are the man she's been waiting for all her life.

How To Make A Woman Trust You Completely

I'm about to reveal a little-known secret of human persuasion that can induce the woman to feel complete trust for you, and have sex with you... even if it's the very first date.

You see, for a woman to have sex with a guy, she must not only be attracted to him, but she must also trust him. Look at it like this:

- Trust Without Attraction = "He's a great friend and I love him to death!" (Translation: "We'll NEVER have sex!")
- Attraction Without Trust = "I'm not a loose woman. He'll have to wait before he gets any!"

However, if the woman has both attraction AND trust for the guy, she'll be literally begging you to take her home with you that night.

Let's take a typical scenario. Say it's coming up on 11 PM, and you've been with a woman since 6 that afternoon. As long as you've had good rapport with her and you've kept pushing the interaction forward, you can assume she's attracted to you.

And by the way, with a woman, you should always assume attraction until proven otherwise. Because the bottom line is that as long as you've got good body language, you've got a lot going on in your life, and you're witty and interesting, she WILL be attracted to you.

Now you need to build trust. By the time you finish this article, you'll know an easy, efficient way to do that.

And by the way, this is a one of the best-kept secrets of human persuasion. The most successful advertisers and salesmen to make billions use it, and now you'll be able to use it with women.

Have you ever noticed how ads will sometimes mention minor defects in the products? A famous example of this was the wildly success Volkswagen Beetle ads from 30 years ago that had the huge headline: "Lemon."

The point of the ad was that not all of their cars were perfect. VW took its quality inspections so seriously that it took note of even small weaknesses in the builds of its cars.

You see, if a person tells you something that's against his self-interest, you tend to trust him more.

We all do. It's a fundamental trait of human psychology.

So when it comes to women, you should point out your minor flaws. Examples could be:

- "I have an ugly mole on my neck. Sometimes I feel self-conscious about it."
- "I had to give a speech last week and felt so nervous!"
- "I don't always floss my teeth even though I should."

Even if they're fake flaws, it doesn't necessarily matter. By pointing them out, you create a perception of honesty within the woman.

Because she believes the minor imperfections about you, she'll believe the MAJOR PERFECTIONS about you as well.

This means that, having both attraction for AND trust in you, later that night she could be breathlessly panting, "I've never done it with a guy this soon before!"

The Number One Secret Behind the Alpha Male's Body Language

Watch a man with high status--Brad Pitt, George Clooney, or the CEO where you work--and you'll notice that he moves differently than the rest of us. He gives off vibes that he is hot stuff, and because of that, women get soaking wet over him.

You, too, can create that aura that makes you attractive to women.

Have you ever noticed the way your friends look when they're all nervous? They're looking down at the ground with their arms crossed, fidgeting, with their voices cracking and their eyes bugged out.

And when you give off that kind of body language yourself, women don't want to be around you.

Now, think about successful guys. They've got girls all over them and some great body language going on.

So, what's the number one secret between those high status guys and the low status guys? You've probably guessed it... the alpha males are relaxed and in control when it comes to social situations.

Make no mistake about it... relaxation is the most important mental state for you to be in.

With that in mind, here are some pointers for you to develop the mindset and body language of an alpha male (and by the way, if you think they're easy, you're right... you can make these changes as early as tonight and have even the hottest girls clamoring for your attention):

1. **Don't allow yourself to feel worried**. Just let your worries go, since you can't solve any problem by worrying. So suck it up, and quit thinking about what might go wrong. Just live life.

   Now, I know what I just said is easier said than done (to use an old--but relevant in this case--cliche). You've spent your whole life up until now dwelling on thoughts that make you feel worried.

   But what is this emotion we call "worry"? When you think about it, it's simply the fear of what might happen in the future. Essentially you're punishing yourself by feeling upset before anything bad has happened. It makes no logical sense to worry!

   So the solution is to avoid contemplating your worrisome thoughts anymore. Identify them for what they are... toxic to your emotional state, and... let them go.

   Simply not dwelling on negative outcomes that make you feel upset will reduce 90% of your worries.

2. A second strategy to relax is to **breathe through your abdomen rather than your chest**.

   When you breathe, imagine that you're bringing air down to your stomach. Feel your belly rise and fall as you breathe.

3. **Avoid nonverbal behaviors** that are the opposite of relaxation:
    - Raising your shoulders.
    - Wrinkling your forehead.
    - Fidgeting with your hands and/or legs.
    - Tightening your facial muscles.

4. **Relax all your muscles** and slow down all of your movements a notch.

    Alpha males generally move unhurriedly, as if they are in control of time itself. Beta males are nervous and make jerky movements. Imagine you are standing and walking through a swimming pool, where your movements are slow and fluid.

5. **Relax your eyes and eyelids**.

    Beta males hold their eyelids wide open because they are so nervous. Their eyes dart all around. Instead let your eyelids rest. Look straight ahead. Only give things your attention if they interest you. While you're out and about, do the affirmation to yourself, "I am sexual, I am relaxed, and I am in control."

6. **If someone wants your attention, move your head slowly**.

    A trait common to many beta males is being so eager to please that when someone calls their name, you see them spin their heads toward the person unnaturally fast.

How To Have Sex On The First Date

Having gone out with literally thousands of women and gone to bed with hundreds over the past two and a half decades, I've learned that there's nothing you can do to GUARANTEE having sex with any particular woman.

However, by doing a few simple things, you can dramatically INCREASE THE ODDS of going all the way on the very first night of your relationship.

1. **Meet her in a non-traditional venue**.

By that I mean, don't take her to a fancy dinner or do anything else that she associates with a "date." If you do, that puts her into the same "make him wait" mindset that she adopted with the last 100 guys who bought her a nice dinner.

Instead meet her somewhere informal, like a coffee shop or some cheap diner for lunch. Don't make a big deal out of who pays for what, because again, the last 100 guys she dated paid for her meal because, as was blatantly obvious to her, they were hoping to get laid.

As an alpha male, you shouldn't do anything because you're "hoping to get laid." That reeks of desperation and kills attraction that a woman feels.

A more attractive guy is one who gets laid all the time, so sex is no big deal to him. If a woman wants his attention, she has to earn it. In other words, he is a challenge for her, not a sure thing.

2. Have the proper mindset throughout the date.

You want to be relaxed and feeling sexual. (To get yourself into a sexual state, try watching porn just before the date, but don't masturbate.) And it's important to feel relaxed. No nervousness.

For a woman to become sexual, she needs to feel relaxed and horny. It is important that you feel that exact way yourself, because studies have shown that when two people are in rapport, they eventually match emotional states with each other.

So when you're chilling with the girl, you should feel deeply relaxed and horny, and then engage her in conversation about neutral subjects until you see signs that she too is getting relaxed and horny.

3. Get her alone with you.

Let's say you and the girl hit it off fantastically in the coffee shop, so you then take her to a bar to get a quick drink. Things are really going well there. The conversational vibe is excellent. You see signs of her increasing sexual arousal and openness to intimacy.

Some signs of a woman's deepening sexual attraction to you include: - Sitting with her inner thigh exposed.
  - Fidgeting with her clothes. She might even unfasten a button or two of her blouse.

- She engages in "triangle gazing." She'll look at one of your eyes, then another, and then at your mouth.
- You notice her stealing glimpses at your chest and even your crotch.

The problem is you can't just say, "Let's go to my place and have sex." With women you're on a first date with, whenever you verbalize anything sexual, it kills the mood for her and results in you sleeping alone that night.

Instead, mention an innocent excuse for the two of you to go to your place. (Examples could be, "You should come hear my 'Best of the 80s' CD" or "That's awesome that you're so good with art... I have a painting in my living room that I'd love to get your opinion on").

Since the two of you have an "innocent" reason to be alone together, it avoids triggering the alarm bells in her mind that scream, "Uh oh! I don't want to be a slut!"

Once the two of you are then alone, isolated at your place, you can set the scene for the seduction.

It can take several hours for the woman to feel comfortable enough with you at your house, so you need to be patient.

Sit on your couch and watch a movie. Slowly escalate. Hold hands, stroke her hair, and so on from there.

Sexually, women are like irons. They heat up slowly. Keep that in mind and don't rush things, and you'll have your maximum shot at having sex on a first date.